OUR FLAG

By Carl Memling
Illustrated by Stephen Cook

 A GOLDEN BOOK • NEW YORK

Every country has its own flag.

When a ship at sea flies our flag, the ship is saying, "I come from America."

When you carry our flag, you are saying, "I am an American."

But our flag did not always look the way it looks today. . . .

Once, a long time ago, the people of America had many different flags. They lived in thirteen separate colonies. And each colony had its own flag.

This boy's flag meant "I am from Maryland."

Maryland was only one part of the big country that
was to be the United States of America.

The thirteen colonies were ruled by the king of England. They did not like being ruled by a king who lived so far away. They wanted to rule themselves. But first they had to fight a war against the British.

In the early days of the Revolutionary War, the Americans still carried their old flags into battle.

They needed one flag that would stand for all the Americans fighting for freedom together.

A drawing was made.

It showed a flag colored red, white, and blue. There were thirteen red and white stripes. And thirteen white stars on a field of blue.

The American flag was to have a star and a stripe for each one of the thirteen colonies.

Who sewed our first flag? No one really knows. But some people believe it was Betsy Ross.

They say she took some bolts of cloth, and cut thirteen red and white stripes. She cut thirteen white stars and one large square of blue. And then Betsy Ross began to sew. . . .

At last the first Stars and Stripes was finished.
"It is a beautiful flag," said General George
Washington when he saw it.

The new flag was carried into battle for the first time when the American ship *Ranger* met a British warship at sea. It was a hard fight, but the *Ranger* won.

The American soldiers fought many battles against the British. The last one was at Yorktown in Virginia. The Americans had won the war.

Now the world had a new country—the United States of America.

The new country began to grow. Two new states joined it. And two more stars and two more stripes were added to the flag.

Then the United States and England fought the War of 1812. . . .

The brand-new flag, with fifteen stars and fifteen stripes, waved over Fort McHenry, near Baltimore, Maryland. All through the night British warships fired their cannon at the fort.

But the flag did not go down. The American soldiers would not surrender. And they won the battle.

Every country has its own song. Our country's song is "The Star-Spangled Banner."

It tells the story just told here—the story of the flag that was still flying when morning came at Fort McHenry.

More states joined the country. But more stripes on the flag would have made it look too crowded. Something had to be done.

It was decided that the flag should always have thirteen stripes—one for each of the thirteen original colonies.

Every time a new state joined, another star was added to the flag.

Our country grew very quickly. When the American people saw how many stars their flag soon had, they were very proud.

Then a war broke out between the states of the North and the states of the South. The soldiers of the South carried their own flag into battle. It was called the Flag of the Confederacy.

The North won the war. And again the country had one flag—the Stars and Stripes!

America grew and grew. At last it had forty-eight states. Now the flag had forty-eight stars. This was when your great-great-grandfather was a boy.

Many years later, during World War II, American marines won a famous battle on an island called Iwo Jima. The year was 1945, and the victory flag they raised still had forty-eight stars.

Thirteen years after Iwo Jima, in 1958, Alaska became the forty-ninth state.

The next year, in 1959, Hawaii became the fiftieth state.

Today our flag has fifty stars—one star for each of the fifty states. And it has thirteen stripes—one for each of the thirteen original colonies.

The stars and stripes of our flag tell the story of America—from the very start until today.

Follow these rules when you carry or fly the flag.

Hold the flag high. Do not let it touch the ground, the floor, or water.

When hanging the flag flat against a wall, the union must be on top and to the flag's own right.

Fly it at the very top of the pole, with the blue square, known as the union, on top.

Take it down at sunset, and fold it neatly.

There are three special times when the flag must be saluted.

When you see it being raised or lowered.

When you are singing "The Star-Spangled Banner."

When the flag passes by in a parade.

When you salute the flag, stand as straight as you can.

A boy takes off his hat and holds it over his heart with his right hand.

A girl leaves her hat on. But she holds her right hand over her heart.

A pledge is a promise. When boys and girls at school pledge their allegiance to the flag, they promise to be good Americans.

THE PLEDGE OF ALLEGIANCE

"I pledge allegiance
to the Flag of the United States of America
and to the Republic
for which it stands;
one nation under God,
indivisible,
with liberty and justice for all."